LEADERSHIP LESSONS LEARNED FROM THE PEOPLE
OF NEWFOUNDLAND, CANADA, IN THE AFTERMATH OF 9/11

LEADING FROM THE STOP

POSITIVE INFLUENCE AND HEARTFELT RESILIENCE IN TIMES OF ADVERSITY

ELIAS KANARIS

AVIVA PUBLISHING
New York

Leading From The Stop:
Positive Influence and Heartfelt Resilience in Times of Adversity

Copyright © 2021 by Elias Kanaris. All rights reserved.

Published by:
Aviva Publishing
Lake Placid, NY
(518) 523-1320
www.AvivaPubs.com

All Rights Reserved. No part of this book may be used or reproduced in any manner whatsoever without the expressed written permission of the author. Address all inquiries to:

Elias Kanaris
Phone: +64 9 280 4420
Email: info@EliasKanaris.com
www.LeadingFromTheStop.com

ISBN: 978-1-63618-140-0 (paperback)
ISBN: 978-1-63618-141-7 (ePub)

Library of Congress Control Number: 2021913477

Editor: Ruth Murray
Cover Designer and Interior Book Layout: Roland Meissner/Love Your Brand
Cover Photo: Gander Airport Search and Rescue
Author Photo: Roland Meissner/Love Your Brand

Every attempt has been made to source properly all quotes.

Printed in New Zealand

First Edition

International listing: Ingram Spark August 2021 (Wild Side Publishing)

DEDICATION

To the people of Newfoundland, Canada. In my heart you will always be affectionately known as 'Newfies'. What you did to set up a safe and welcoming space for us 'plane people', shows us that there is a positive side to humanity.

In particular, the residents of the towns of Gander and Gambo. You searched your pantries, raided your fridges and emptied your freezers to meet our needs. But most importantly you opened your hearts and poured out unconditional love. You taught us that you could drop everything that you were planning to do and pivot at a moment's notice, without the need for a detailed plan, just a selfless urge to help others in need.

To the leadership and congregation of the Salvation Army (SA), Gambo, thank you for providing us with shelter in a storm. There are far too many of you to mention individually, however, you will be remembered through the heroics of Theresa Antonietti (nee Burry) who became the face of the SA. Your compassion and genuine love for others shone through the darkness. You taught us that relationships were important and how to look out for the individual.

Finally, on behalf of the crew and wider team of United Airlines, Captain Mike Ballard. You provided leadership that empowered us and kept us safe. From the first announcement that you made on the flight, alerting us to an event that would change the world, you modelled leadership. Instead of filling us with fear, you gave us hope. In my mind you were saying three key things:

Nothing's wrong
You were here to help us
You believed in us

Your daily briefings were compassionate, without being sugar coated. In a time of adversity, you provided courageous leadership when it was needed the most. As John Maxwell states, you taught us that leadership was influence; nothing more, nothing less.

Thank you to you all for having a positive impact on my life, as well as the other 197 passengers of flight UA929 when our lives crossed on that fateful Tuesday in September, 2001.

ACKNOWLEDGEMENTS

No book is written alone, so I would like to thank the many people who have influenced my journey:

Andy Rolston, Belinda Hendricks, Bill James, Bob Smith, Cam Calkoen, Captain Mike Ballard, Chad Johnson, Claude Elliott, Craig Fisher, Gilly Chater, Jason Brook, John Barley, Jon Dunning, Jonna Hunt, Julian Dawson, Kimberly Whetsell, Laine Zizka, Linda Perry, Lindsay Adams OAM, Mark Cole, Martin Brooker, Dr. Mary C. Kelly, Mike Handcock, Montiano (Monti) Blom, Natasha Gagarin, Patrick Snow, Rabia Siddique, Samantha Watkins, Sheri Griffin, Theresa Antoinetti, Yvonne Godfrey.

I would also like to thank six more people who were all very influential in making this project work. Craig Fisher for publishing and maintaining the original website (UA929.org) that caught our experiences in a snapshot in time. Ruth Murry for her support and help in guiding me during the editing of this manuscript. Roland Meissner for his expertise in graphic design. You brought my vision of this book to life. Patrick Snow for his enthusiasm and support as my publishing coach. The Holy Spirit, who encouraged me to write the framework of this book in less than three weeks, following nearly two decades of research. And finally, my wife, Kay Kanaris, you were my biggest cheerleader, and without your expertise, this book may never have been birthed.

CONTENTS:

FOREWORD - By Mark Cole	ix
REFERENCE - Introduction	01
REDEFINE - The Wardrobe Malfunction	05
RESPOND - The Panicked Crew	09
REMOTE - The Night On The Tarmac	15
REVELATION – The Conversation with The Passenger from Zoo	21
RELEASE - The Disembarkation	27
RELATIONSHIPS - The Sallies, The Pews & The Camp Beds	31
REFOCUS - The Food, The Entertainment and The Daily Updates	37
REALIGN - The Funeral & The Escape Committee	43
RELAX - The Messages (From) Home	47
REDEFINE - The Roles of the Locals	55
REFRESH – Showering at Someone's Home	63
RECOGNITION – Paying Attention to Individuals (The Married Couple and The Campbells)	69
RESET - The Call To Return To The Plane	77
RELIEF - The Emotion of Chicago	83
REDRESS - Correcting the Wardrobe Malfunction	89
RECOLLECTIONS - In Their Own Words	93
REFLECTING - A Final Thought	97
ABOUT THE AUTHOR	103
WHERE TO FROM HERE	106
ENDNOTES	108

LEADING FROM THE STOP

FOREWORD

by Mark Cole

Where do you turn for leadership wisdom?

That's a simple question with a complicated answer, depending on who you ask, of course. For over 20 years I've worked alongside Dr. John C. Maxwell, recognized by many as the number one leadership expert in the world. Plenty of people turn to John for his leadership wisdom, be it through his books, his podcast, or his speaking events. For over 40 years John has worked hard to build credibility as a leader so people would trust him and come to him for help.

In fact, it's through John Maxwell and my work as his CEO that I met Elias Kanaris, the author of this book. Elias was one of the first people to join John's coaching company, The John Maxwell Team—and when I say one of the first, I mean it: he was the fourth or fifth person to plunk down a cheque to learn leadership from one of the world's best leaders and teachers.

But for as much as Elias learned from John, that's not where he turned for the wisdom found in this book.

Instead, Elias leaned into his experience with the Newfies—the nickname for the incredible citizens of Newfoundland, Canada. Elias spent five incredible, unplanned days as an unofficial citizen of Newfoundland when his plane was grounded in the aftermath of 9/11. While the world struggled to comprehend the chaos of unspeakable terror, Elias gleaned incredible insights from the people around him who sought to bring order and comfort to the chaos.

That's a pretty good description of leadership, actually: bringing order and comfort out of chaos. It's a little old-fashioned, I suppose, but it's something people are missing from the leadership they experience these days. Maybe it's because leadership has shifted its focus from people to production; we're in such a hurry to get things done that we neglect the very people who accomplish the things we need done.

As CEO of a leadership training company, that loss of focus challenges me, which is why I'm so excited for Elias's book. Having known him now for nearly a decade and having followed his incredible work with the Global Speakers Federation, I am confident that the lessons he learned those five days in Newfoundland will point you to a powerful philosophy of values-based, people centric, servant leadership.

Because that's what he saw in action. He knows first-hand that it works, and he wants to share its power to transform you, your team, or your organization.

Read this book carefully from cover to cover. In fact, read through it a couple of times: the first time, mark up the book with your notes and thoughts; the second time, let the book mark you with its wisdom and truth. That's how the best leaders read, and it's how a book truly imparts its full lesson. I've read Elias's book, and I promise you it will help you, enlighten you, and make you a better leader, the kind others want to follow.

You may never have considered Newfoundland, Canada as a wellspring of leadership wisdom, but that's okay. Elias has, and he's put those profound lessons into this wonderfully enjoyable book that I wholeheartedly recommend.

Enjoy your read and keep your eyes open—you never know when a leadership lesson will unfold before you.

Let's listen, let's learn, and let's lead people the way they deserve to be led.

All the best,

Mark Cole

CEO/President
The John Maxwell Enterprise

LEADING FROM THE STOP

REFERENCE

Introduction

It was an ordinary Tuesday. I was in town for a meeting when my phone buzzed. Waiting till my meeting had finished, I checked and saw that it was a text from my wife, Kay asking: "R u available sometime this arvo for a meeting with Darrell?" This was not a good message to receive.

"Darrell", to whom the text referred, was the principal of the high school that my children attended.

I went through the mental checklist. My two eldest daughters as adults, living in Christchurch, were discounted out of the equation. Of my two younger children, my daughter had already graduated high school and was due to start at university. That only left my youngest – my son Nicholas.

I tried calling my wife, but each call ended in voicemail prison, so with a sense of disappointment and anxiety, I texted her back. "Sounds ominous. Just tried to call your mobile and your office number. Please call me when you're able."

When you get invited to attend a meeting with your child's principal, you know that something is up. I ran through a series of potential reasons in my mind... Was there a fight? Did someone get hurt? Was there spilling of blood involved?

By the time we entered the Principal's office a few hours later, we were reassured that Nicholas was not in trouble. The reason that we were asked in was that one of his teachers had noticed that he was rather lethargic and become disconnected in the classroom. Nicholas had fallen back in his contributions and wanting to help him, she instigated a meeting with Nicholas and the Principal.

During this initial meeting, Nicholas was asked if his attention was being distracted by his smartphone. He acknowledged that he was using it for Instagram, YouTube and the like, but hadn't connected this with his changed engagement in class. When challenged on how much time he was spending on his device, Nicholas estimated it to be between 60 – 90 minutes. The 'Digital Wellbeing' report on his phone revealed that it was between five and six hours per day!

Principal Darrell's youngest son was in the same class as Nicholas and it transpired it was common amongst young adults that they drastically underestimated the amount of time they actually spent on their smartphones. Having taken his son through a similar conversation, Darrell helped Nicholas to become aware that the gulf between perception and reality were immense.

Our meeting with Darrell concluded as he pointed us towards some strategies and Apps that we could install onto Nicholas's smartphone to help him manage, control and monitor the amount of time he spent online.

When we returned home that evening, Kay and I arranged for Nicholas to join us in my home office, where we had a heartfelt conversation. Sitting around the coffee table, Nicholas in the armchair directly in front of me and Kay to my left and Nicholas's right.

I cleared my throat, and said, "Nicholas, let me kick off by stating three things. Number 1 – you're not in trouble. Number two – we believe in you. And number three – we're here to help." I knew that it was important to frame our conversation and to ensure that Nicholas knew that he was in a safe space.

We talked through the issues and came to an agreement that Nicholas would allow us to download the App onto his phone, limiting his screen time to a maximum of an hour a day, Monday through Friday and 2 hours on the weekend.

There was a sense of relief from Nicholas as he acknowledged that he had been feeling like he had had little control regulating his behaviour and his emotions. What had been set in place would aid him with this and drawing the meeting to its natural conclusion, I re-iterated to Nicholas that there were three things:

REFERENCE

1) You're not in trouble
2) We believe in you
3) We're here to help

As he left, my mind was drawn back to another Tuesday, nearly 18 years earlier, where I heard a similar message. It started off with the sentence, *"Ladies and gentlemen, let me first reassure you that there is nothing wrong with this plane..."*

LEADING FROM THE STOP

REDEFINE

The Wardrobe Malfunction

Imagine waking up today and realising that you had a wardrobe malfunction. Would it impact you? Would it change your life forever? Would it end up changing you?

It was an ordinary Tuesday, uneventful so far apart from THAT wardrobe malfunction. As I got changed into my suit at my parent's house in Wimbledon, South London, I realised that I had not packed a tie!

I know, I can hear you cry, "But Elias, not having a tie ISN'T a wardrobe malfunction!" It certainly was in the bygone time I am sharing about. It was when flying business class required a certain decorum, this was an era where you were expected to dress for the part.

I kissed my mum goodbye and gave my dad a hug while the taxi driver put my bags into the back of his cab. Soon I was in the taxi and heading towards Heathrow Airport, where upon arriving I made a detour via the Tie Rack (that should help date this story!) to purchase the requisite tie before heading into the United Airlines Business Club Lounge.

With my new tie securely fastened, I took a leisurely stroll and proceeded to the departure gate where I was welcomed on board and waved through to my seat at the head of the business class cabin.

The flight was UA929, heading to Chicago, where I was due to present at a conference.

The date was September 11, 2001.

Nothing could have prepared anyone for the tragedies that were about to occur. Halfway through our flight, just after the crew cleared away our lunch, my world would be abruptly changed forever. I'm still unsure whether it was the panicked look on the faces of the crew as they scurried around the plane or the horrendous sound that I heard alerting me to an issue. I later found out that the noise was caused by a combination of jettisoning fuel, in anticipation of our imminent touchdown, and the premature deployment of the landing gear to slow the speed of the plane.

While we were quickly reassured by Captain Mike Ballard that there was nothing wrong with the plane, due to a "significant incident in the United States," all airspace within it had been closed. As a precaution, our plane was being diverted and we were going to be landing in Gander, which was in Newfoundland, Canada.

To be honest, I had no idea where that was, and my mind started to race. What was that 'significant incident'? My first thought was that the President of the USA had been assassinated; that was quickly overtaken by another – maybe there was a nuclear attack on US soil. I arched my neck to look past my fellow passenger who occupied the window seat. Would I be able to see a mushroom cloud through the window out to the horizon?

Thankfully, I couldn't see anything. The next 30 minutes were spent preparing the plane for its unscheduled early landing. The crew cleared away all the remnants of our lunch, eradicating any evidence of normality in this flight. What was supposed to be an eight-and-a-half-hour flight had been cut by half.

A hush fell upon the plane; passengers and crew alike assumed a sombre attitude. Soon the tell-tale signs of descent were felt as the barometric pressure drop caused me to swallow till my ears 'popped' and the discomfort in my ears disappeared.

Our plane continued to lose altitude and soon we were touching down. We had indeed been diverted to Gander Airport, Newfoundland, affectionately known by its airport code 'YQX'. We were one of thirty-eight planes grounded there as a result of the 9/11 terrorist attacks.

My earlier wardrobe malfunction was no longer as significant as it had seemed prior to boarding as I prepared to disembark.

TIME TO REFLECT...

What is your first recollection of 9/11?

Where were you and how did you hear about it?

How have the images of the planes crashing into the twin towers had an impact on you?

9/11 was devastating. Lives were lost, families were torn apart and industries like airlines came to a crashing halt overnight with many people losing their livelihoods.

Media reports drew a grey cloud of doom and gloom over the economy. Parallels were being made to the Great Depression. Yet, despite the doomsayers, communities rallied to help each other and we eventually emerged from this catastrophe.

What are some of the lessons learned through this and similar experiences?

LEADING FROM THE STOP

RESPOND

The Panicked Crew

When you fly business class, you have certain benefits. We were amongst the first to board the plane, had more leg room and the seats were wider. There were fewer passengers in the business class section and your meal trays seemed to be bigger, reflective of the extensive menu selection in comparison to guests in economy.

I remember sitting at the front of the business class section. The seat arrangement on the Boeing 777 was 2-3-2. I think that I was in row 7, in the aisle seat. Next to me was a passenger who occupied the window seat. I'm sure that his journey had started deep inside India, possibly some 36 hours prior to joining me on this flight. We exchanged the usual business class greetings, which consisted of a grunt to acknowledge each other.

My mind was already pre-occupied and all I wanted to do was to get settled in, prepare a message to send through to my wife, have lunch, and work on my report. The last thing that I needed was to be distracted by my fellow passengers.

Lunch was eventually served, and I interrupted my work to eat. My laptop was powered down and stored away so my table could change function to accommodate the tray containing my lunch. I couldn't tell you what I ate, only that I probably washed it down with a coffee.

As soon as the crew cleared the meal trays, I proceeded to revert my tray back to its intended purpose – support my laptop as I continued to write the note to update my wife on what was happening at my parents' house.

You have to remember that these were the days when there wasn't any WiFi on an airplane. We did not live in an instantly and constantly connected world. My note, which was probably written in a Microsoft Word document, would become an attachment that I intended to send once I had settled into my hotel room in Chicago.

Unfortunately, despite my best intentions, this plan was never going to see the light of day.

Not long after lunch, I noticed that something was amiss. I think it was the initial panicked look amongst the crew as they scurried around that first alerted me to an issue. This was confirmed by Captain Mike Ballard's message to us all. He was soon to be referred to by us affectionately as Capt. Mike.

What then pursued was a sense of composed activity. I don't have any recollection of panic amongst the passengers and certainly no panic in my soul. Even 20 years later, I look back at that part of the episode and think that to all intents and purposes things were 'normal'.

Reflecting, I would say that was in a large part due to:
1) Capt. Mike's calmness in giving us transparency and reassurance about our situation ("a significant incident... but that there was nothing wrong with the plane..."), and
2) The crew confidently going through their routine procedures associated with a landing.

Because the crew drew on their training and commenced preparing the plane, it was apparent that we were going to land somewhere and soon. It just wasn't going to be our initial destination, Chicago.

I was one of a number of passengers, locals and cast members from the musical 'Come From Away' that were interviewed in 2020 about my experiences by Laine Zizka for her Master of Science in Communication Studies thesis. As I read through her thesis, I was drawn by a comment made by another passenger, Jodi Taub. She recalled the moment that she knew something was wrong.

> *As our plane was approaching the East Coast, instead of going left for North America, it took a right. At that point, we had seen on the screen that our flight was going back out to the ocean, which was disconcerting to everybody. More so than anything else, I knew something was wrong.*[1]

It doesn't matter what the trigger was for each and every passenger (and I'm sure that you could interview all 198 on our plane and still receive 198 differing accounts), that was the point that our collective lives would change. Zizka, in her thesis, articulates it perfectly: "While the passengers expressed feelings of uncertainty, the crews [sic] were grappling how to handle the news while processing it themselves."[1]

The crew's ability to perform their duties whilst under untold pressure is a testament to their ability to lead. I am convinced that as a direct result of the instructions passed to them from Capt. Mike, through chief purser Natasha Gagarin, the flight crew was able to instil calm and confidence that we were in good hands.

When life throws you a curveball, what are you going to do? Will you fall apart at the seams, or will you fall back on preset systems and processes? Do you have a Plan B? Have you documented a recovery plan for yourself, your family, your business and/or your community?

The crew of UA929 were trained to deal with many eventualities. Engine failures. Crash landings. Turbulence. Even medical incidents. The next time that you face a crisis, remember that if you are the leader, all the eyes of your followers will be trained on you. Your response to the crisis will either inspire or dishearten them.

TIME TO REFLECT...

Oz Fudge, a Royal Canadian Mounted Police (RCMP) Officer stated, "Our emergency plan would deal with fires, would deal with plane crashes, would deal with anything along those lines. But, we had nothing – and I believe I said this on the Today show – we had nothing where seven thousand people would drop in for a bucket of tea and a bicky."[1]

As part of your day-to-day operations, do you include emergency planning? What would happen if a disaster affected you today? How would you cope? Would you become a victim or a victor?

Who is in your inner circle, the people who you can turn to and trust when you need help? Are you meeting with them on a regular basis already?

When Covid-19 hit, how did you respond, or did you react? Given your situation, have you made any changes to the way that you are now preparing for the unexpected? If not and you recognise that you need to, when will you be starting and what will assist you to?

RESPOND

REMOTE

The Night On The Tarmac

The plane touched down with a jolt. After we landed and taxied the plane to a halt on the tarmac, where we were joined by a number of other planes, some parked at an angle to accommodate more as they arrived.

I remember that it was then that Capt. Mike started to explain what had happened. He gave us a brief overview of the terrorist attacks and mentioned that the twin towers in NYC had been hit. Whilst the initial details were sketchy, he promised to give us more transparency. This was going to be delivered via the BBC World service, which he promised would be available on one of the entertainment channels as soon as he was able to patch it in.

On another flight, Kerry Derringer-Cashin, who was a passenger on the first plane to touch down, made the following observation after the crew told them what had happened:

> *They finally told us and everybody just kind of went quiet. This is an act of war. But we still kind of didn't quite grasp what was going on because we were just sitting among ourselves on the airplane. We had no radio, no video, even the flight attendants in the crew didn't know what was going on. It wasn't just that they weren't telling us, they didn't know either... I felt like I was in a World War II movie because it was like this staticky connection, it's dark, we're all standing around listening to it.*[1]

We, at least had the BBC World service piped in. I was still in a state of disbelief. My mind raced as I thought about my family back in New Zealand. It would have been early in the morning back in Auckland. Maybe 2 or 3 am?

There was an airphone in the seat that I was occupying, and I decided to make a long-distance call to ensure my wife was not alarmed about my safety. I swiped my credit card down the length of the phone and dialled my home number. After what seemed like an eternity, the call would not connect and all I could hear were the beeping tones of the international 'busy' signal from the carrier. I tried multiple times. Each returned the same result.

Eventually I tried my parents back in London and was able to speak with my mum.

I reassured her that I was safe and asked her to connect with other family members. I might have spoken to my uncle in New Jersey, or my brother or sister in Connecticut to let them know I was safe and to confirm that they were. Each call would have only lasted a few moments.

Over the next 3 or 4 hours, in between listening to the BBC World service and receiving sporadic updates from Capt. Mike, I continued to try calling home. Eventually, I was rewarded with a ringing tone. Kay answered the phone after several rings. My call had woken her up. She was totally unaware of what had happened in New York City. Our daughter, Brianna, who would have been about 5 months old at the time, was still asleep.

I asked Kay if she had heard the news, which she hadn't. I encouraged her not to panic and tried to explain what I knew of the situation. Most importantly, I wanted her to know that I was safe. Before the end of our call, she had switched on the TV. It would have been about 6:30am in New Zealand by this stage.

I went on to explain that I expected us to be given the all-clear within a short time frame. At this time I was fully convinced that we would be back in the air and on our way to Chicago soon. Talk about naivety!

Was I in denial? Absolutely. Was I aware of that? No.

Many of you will be aware that there are multiple models that talk about the different stages of grief. One of these models refers to five stages. Does grief always follow the same order of stages? Not always.

This model identifies the five stages of grief as:

- denial
- anger
- bargaining
- depression
- acceptance

I was wallowing in the first stage. In fact, I don't think that I got past that stage for a long time.

Seconds ticked into minutes, which soon turned into hours. We were told that we would be remaining in our plane while the airport authority put in place an immigration and security screening infrastructure. That indicated that we would be disembarking and going somewhere. I thought that meant it would be happening soon.

Thankfully, Capt. Mike was able to update us at regular intervals. Soon we encountered our first challenge on board the plane. The air-conditioning system on the plane failed. A passenger on our flight, Steve, wrote about his experiences to his friends. We were lucky enough to capture this for posterity in a website that Craig Fisher, a fellow plane person, set up. I'll let Steve set up the scene:

> *During the first day the AC malfunctioned (it was 84 degrees outside) so they opened all of the doors. We joked about the temptation to jump and make a run for it but it was a long way down to the tarmac... and we didn't want to get shot. One good thing for us was that we were on a big plane. The "Triple-7", as they call it, is very large aircraft with two aisles and room to stroll. Another good thing was that the plane was only about 75 percent full. Most of the time our wait was extremely boring but we were just fortunate to be on the ground and not one of the planes into an American skyscraper.*[2]

We were told that they would have to open the doors to allow some air to flow. This was accompanied with an (obvious) safety instruction not to venture next to the opened doors.

Despite the fact that we were living in a bygone era where common sense was more common than it seems to be today, we needed some boundaries to be put into place. I would suggest that this is a good lesson for leaders who need to lead from the stop...

TIME TO REFLECT...

During times of adversity, you will need to have a communications plan. It might be worth writing down a list of people, with their accompanying contact details and keeping it in a safe place with easy access. That might be online (in a cloud based storage system) or in hardcopy (if you're more old-school). Or even both!

Once created, it would be worthwhile updating the list from time to time. Phone numbers change. New people enter the scene and have to be added to the updates list.

The other risk is being in denial of your situation. It will take a cool head and level-headed thinking to allow you to navigate the first couple of hours or days after a crisis hits.

If you are in a leadership position, remember that all eyes will be focused on you. You will need to stay calm and lead...

REVELATION

The Conversation with The Passenger from Zoo

As the day wore on, we were encouraged to stretch our legs. What previously had been the demarcation between classes in the plane, was soon discarded. The toilets within the business class section were opened for all passenger use. The practicality of this new environment meant that we had to adapt. We could not be expected to continue with our predefined boundaries. We needed to adjust and redefine our world.

Soon we found ourselves walking within the confines of the plane. Before I realised it, I was acknowledging other passengers as they stood next to me in the aisle, patiently waiting their turn to use the business class toilets.

Day turned to dusk and soon it turned into night.

We had received the remainder of the food that was on board. The crew issued us with instructions that we were running low on water and encouraged us to economise wherever possible. Blankets were distributed and passengers turned in for the night, squirming on their chair trying to secure a more comfortable position in the hope of getting some sleep.

I found myself at the back of the plane, standing next to an American gentleman and we struck up a conversation. I remember him saying something to the effect of, "Why would anybody want to attack the USA?" I found his comment interesting. I asked him whether he was aware of the US foreign policy and the potential impact that it might have had on other countries.

He seemed very adamant in his view that the US had never caused any issues, acting in the role of big brother to help other nations during their time of trouble. As a person who was born in Tripoli, Libya, brought up in London, England and now living in Auckland, New Zealand, I understood the impact that colonisation could have.

I mentioned that sometimes, despite their initial intentions, the indigenous population were left with a feeling of subjugation. Despite my attempts to make him aware of the impact that colonisation had within the British empire, that undoubtedly led to issues of resentment to the 'Mother Ship', my fellow passenger was not going to be deviated from his viewpoint.

I soon realised that I was not going to win friends and influence people if I continued this conversation. We parted ways and I went back to my seat and tried to get some sleep. Night turned back into day and we awoke to the new dawn, still on our plane, parked at the same angle to the runway.

What I hadn't understood was that during this time, the local community in Gander had mobilised and were putting the infrastructure in place to help accommodate the 6,600-odd passengers and crew that had descended in 38 planes. It turns out that I wasn't the only person in denial. Here's another observation made in Zizka's thesis.

> *While the world was watching the horror unfold in the United States and planes began to land at YQX, Ganderites expressed denial, sure that this diversion would be temporary. Even Brian Mosher, CBC reporter, said all these planes will "be gone tomorrow morning because that was fully expected."*[1]

With American airspace closed, the air traffic controller at YQZ came to the realisation that us 'plane people' would not be going away in a hurry. After their initial sense of disbelief and denial, community members were taking action to prepare the town for the coming crisis. With the state of emergency in place, Gander and the surrounding towns began to coordinate efforts to prepare their homes and spaces for an unknown number of people.

Initially this took the form of security screening and immigration stations that were set up from scratch. Every passenger that was (eventually) disembarked from their plane would have to go through this. It was apparent that the local community would need to host us until American airspace was re-opened.

Following that initial sense of disbelief and denial, the local Newfoundlanders (affectionately called "Newfies") pivoted into swift action, calling on community organisations, like the Salvation Army (SA) and Red Cross. These were quickly overwhelmed, and participants realised they needed to involve public organisations, like the local school.

Everything happened in a matter of three to four hours. They had to get everything ready for the arriving people. Camp beds were set up at a number of public locations.

> *That was going on a [sic] Gander Collegiate. That was going on at St. Paul's College of the North Atlantic. At the churches, at the legion, the Lion's Club, the Elks Club – all these places needed volunteers just like Gander Academy, and it got to the point where they were turning people away.*[1]

TIME TO REFLECT...

Disaster has struck. You may find yourself in an uncomfortable and unusual situation. Potentially you won't have any reference point that you can anchor yourself to regroup before you continue.

The worst potential situation is that you get paralysed into inaction! Straight away, you will need to jump into action.

Don't wait for motivation to kick in. Some of your decisions could have life or death outcomes. Decisive and informed action is important.

If possible, consider who you can turn to to help with the decision-making process. Maybe these are the people on your list that we talked about in the previous chapter. Hopefully you will be aware of their skills and that will help you in the allocation of tasks and activities that can get you out of adversity.

REVELATION

LEADING FROM THE STOP

RELEASE

The Disembarkation

On Wednesday, September 12th, we eventually received word that we were allowed to disembark. Our instructions were simple enough. "Take all your carry-on luggage off with you as you leave the plane."

An airstair was wheeled over and we were asked to leave the plane. It was mid-morning, around 10:30am, and it was chilly and cold as we left the plane. We walked across the tarmac and entered the dated terminal where a makeshift security station had been set up in front of us.

A new set of instructions were constantly being called out for the benefit of new plane people entering the security zone. "Please take out your laptops and switch them on." I would later find out that they were concerned that some of the terrorists were disguising their bombs by hiding them in everyday electronic devices.

I was happy to show my working laptop to the security officer in front of me. With his blessing, I was allowed to power it down, place it back into my carry-on bag and proceed via immigration into the terminal.

There we were greeted by smiling volunteers and tables of donated food. There was a triage organisation in operation, taking down passport numbers, names, home addresses, next of kin, and emergency contact details. In her thesis, Zizka quoted another passenger, Kevin Jung, who clearly remembered his moment of realisation.

> *I took a bite of the KFC and it was ice cold. That doesn't bother me; I love cold chicken, but that's the first time that it hit me that, oh my god, they've been working on this all day. I thought we just couldn't get off*

because they were waiting for clearance or something. But, they had been working all day to prepare for us. We didn't know, at that point, to what extent, but that cold chicken was what snapped me into reality.[1]

By the time our flight was processed, Gander had reached its capacity. We were ushered into yellow school buses and we took a 40-minute ride to the sleepy hollow of Gambo. The buses stopped outside of the Salvation Army (SA) church, this would become our home for the duration of the stop.

I was still uncertain as to the next step and I was convinced that in a couple of hours we would be turning around and going back home. It was about four or five hours into the time at the SA that I was sitting there, thinking, "You know what, maybe I should take my tie off"...

TIME TO REFLECT...

Change always calls for transition. When people are going to make a change, there are parts of the change that they are comfortable with. The fact that they know things will be different and they're usually comfortable with the front end as they begin to prepare for the change.

And they're usually comfortable when they land on the other end, and they have got through the change and settled!

What makes them uncomfortable is the transition.

It's like going to the circus and watching a person on the trapeze go from one set of bars to the other. As long as they are holding on to that first bar, there's a sense of security there. And when they grab hold of the last bar, there's that familiar sense of security again.

But guess what... in between there is some flying going on and they're not holding on to anything and they're asking themselves, "Can I make it?"

I think that's also true for change.

Transition is that period of time when you're asking yourself, "Can I make it?"

Here's what I want you to know. No one has, in baseball, stolen second base without taking their foot off first base! You can't have your foot on first base and stretch 90 feet and have your foot on second base. There's no such thing as being 'safe'. But you can't take second base without taking a risk and without making the transition.

What transition do you need to make right now?

RELATIONSHIPS

The Sallies, The Pews & The Camp Beds

The SA church would end up being our home for the next four days. A fellow passenger, Bob Smith, who, like me, was originally from the UK, wrote an article about what happened whilst we were there. Like fellow plane person, Steve, Bob was able to share his thoughts shortly after we set up the UA929.org website. Here is what Bob wrote:

> *We were greeted at the door by a jovial lady saying, welcome over and over. I learned over the next few days that she, and the other Sally Army people, really meant, welcome.*[3]

They had pulled out all stops to ensure that there was food available for us upon our arrival. The congregants had raided their pantries, their fridges and freezers to lavish home-made food and hospitality on us.

I was overwhelmed. I had a belly full of food and I had taken off my tie, but I was still walking around in my suit, taking in my new surroundings. The sanctuary at the church became the main staging post. People began to mark out their territories. The pews became makeshift beds as individuals started to lie down, attempting to get some much needed rest.

During the day, the Red Cross brought in green camp beds and extra blankets. These were placed into rooms down in the under-belly of the church. I walked into a room which I later found out was their nursery. There were camp beds on the floor and some of them were already spoken for. Thankfully I found the last empty one and claimed it as mine.

The day started to drag on and someone brought a TV into the sanctuary.

With its rabbit ears straining to pick up a signal, it was turned on. Most of the room became mesmerised, watching the footage of the planes slamming into the twin towers. I only watched it once and then left the room.

I didn't want to watch the horror anymore. I was preoccupied with the need to write my report about the trip in Europe and what I had learned. Work HAD to take a priority. All I needed was somewhere peaceful and quiet.

Taking my laptop from the nursery, I entered the main hall, that had been set up as a congregation centre and makeshift restaurant during the day. By this time, dinner had long been served and the space was cleared and almost empty. Sitting close to me was a lovely lady, knitting needles in hand with a cup of tea by her side.

She smiled at me, and I smiled back. Conversation seemed laboured at first as she asked me what I perceived were mundane questions about my family. Was I married? Did I have kids?

It turned out that she was a grandmother to four gorgeous kids. As we were still in an era pre-smartphones, she rummaged through her handbag to find the obligatory passport-sized photo stored in her purse to show me the evidence. At the time all I could think was, "Hurry up, lady, I have to get this report done!" I never did get her name, but in 2018, when I posted an article that I wrote that referenced this experience, a Pastor at SA, Melanie Dawn Rideout, thought that she might have been Melva Warren.

I suppose that she represented a good cross-section of the local Newfies. She seemed content with who she was, and where she was. I suspected that she hadn't travelled much. This was reflected in the note that Steve wrote on our website:

> *I decided to take a poll the second day I was there. I asked one question of almost every Gambo resident I met: "Have you ever left the island?" The answer I got 95 percent of the time was, "No.....why would I ever want to do that? I've never left the island and I never will...especially now". The events in NYC and DC are exactly why they do not want to leave their little part of the planet. To me, the people of Gambo seemed happy. Very happy. And Very kind. Words can't describe them.[4]*

Despite trying my best to kill the conversation, I eventually gave up on my report and shut down my laptop. I drew closer to her and entered the conversation. She was a lovely person and all she wanted to do was to love on me. By this I mean that she wanted to let me know that others, like her, cared about me and she was here if I wanted to talk.

Around 1 am, I thanked her for the conversation and bade her goodnight and went down to the nursery. While I thought that I was being considerate to the other tenants in the room, I must admit that the camp bed squeaked each time I sat on it or turned on my side.

Despite my best efforts, it would appear that I was still too focused on my work. I got up early the next morning and snuck out of the room, thinking that I wasn't disturbing my fellow roommates. It turns out that I was as Bob went on to share in his article:

> *One thing which sticks in my mind was on the second night around 1am, someone came into our room and laid down on the stretcher/cot next to me. He thought he hadn't woken me up. Then at around 5am, up he gets and buggers off. Apparently thinking he hadn't woken anyone up. The next night he comes in again at around 1am and leaves at about 5am. Now you have to remember it's dark and my eyesight even with my glasses isn't that good, so I didn't know who it was. But I did decide that if it happened again I was going to get up and follow this 'Will-o-the-Wisp' to find out who he was and where he was going. I mentioned it to Kifah that morning and he'd seen this chap as well. Do you know who it was? Course you don't. Turns out it's none other than Elias himself. No wonder he had time to build a web site. He has several hours a day more than most of us.*[5]

For the record, Craig Fisher built the website. However, looking back, I can see that I hadn't learned how to relax.

As the week drew to a close, the Newfies interviewed in Zizka's thesis began reflecting on what they had accomplished. Over the course of those days, Claude Elliott, the Mayor of Gander, estimated that the city coordinated 285,000 meals between passengers and volunteers. Karen Mills filled so many beds in the Comfort Inn that she managed and fielded countless loads of laundry for the whole city in the hotel's industrial laundry. But rarely was it about the numbers for the Newfies, as many iterated.

> *I believe Claude has said it a hundred times: When they stepped off the plane they were strangers. By mid-week they were friends. By then end of the week, they were family.*[1]

We started off as strangers. By mid-week we were friends. By the end of the week, we were family...

TIME TO REFLECT...

John Maxwell says that before you ask for a hand, you have to touch a heart. Relationships are more about a heart connection than anything else. Before you buy from somebody you have to get to know, like and trust them. All three components are integral to relationships to some degree or another.

Do you tend to be a task focused individual, or are you more people focused?

At our church, we get out at least once per quarter to undertake a community impact project. During that time, our congregation will mobilise and go to hundreds of homes to bless multiple families/communities. It may mean working in gardens, weeding or cutting back the undergrowth or we could help to clean the inside of homes, halls or schools. Whatever is needed.

Each team has a team leader and a liaison person. The difference is that the team leader tends to be a task focused individual. They will look at the job that has been allocated, and calculate how to split up the job into manageable tasks.

The liaison person has a different focus. Their primary function is to ensure that the individual or family that we are blessing is looked after. It can be traumatic for some of the people that we help to have a group of strangers appear at their doorstep. The liaison person is selected because of their relationship building capabilities.

If you are a task-focused person, who do you have that can be a people-oriented person to support you?

If you are a relationship-focused person, who do you have that can be a task-focused person to support you?

REFOCUS

The Food, The Entertainment and The Daily Updates

Throughout the time that we were staying at the SA, we were constantly fed. There was a big line of trestle tables arranged in the main hall, brimming with food. Breakfast, lunch and dinner.

The hall was rectangular, with a stage at the front end and counterbalanced with a small kitchen at the back. Smaller tables and chairs dotted the walls, allowing us to grab some food and sit in smaller groups together to enjoy the food.

With a stage staring at us, it wasn't long before it too became utilised. One of the passengers, Julian Dawson from the UK, was a musician who was on his way to Nashville to record an album. He became a focal point and in the evening we gathered in front of the stage where he started to entertain us.

The relief that we experienced was a welcome distraction to the otherwise dreary feeling of loneliness. Over time, more people got involved, spreading across the children in our party as well as the Newfies. Another passenger, Tom Cox from Fielding Colorado, captured it well.

> *In the evenings, we sang songs (there was a good guitar player there from the UK on his way to Nashville, Julian Dawson), there were gospel songs sung by the men of the church playing their instruments, some of which were hand made. And Theresa, the church secretary who we began to call Mother Theresa, sang with a group of kids like an old fashion revival. And the young girl choir sang one evening, not too good, but from the heart, our national anthem getting most of the words right and then "O'Canada". These were wonderful experiences...*

> *Hearing those spiritual songs at a time like that was really an inspiration to me and I think gave us all the incentive to reflect on our situation and count our blessings, particularly our families who everybody thought about all the time. We were basically hostages in a friendly environment.*[6]

I love his closing phrase in that article. "We were basically hostages in a friendly environment."

Tom went on to say, "Friendships were forged not only with the others on the plane, but solid friendships as well with the local people there who have such a strong northern accent that sometimes it was hard to understand what they were saying but it was never hard to understand their intentions."[6]

We knew that we were being loved by a group who had their lives rudely interrupted by us. It felt reassuring that we could be allowed to accept our fate without prejudice. Friendships were formed amongst the passengers, across the class segregations, age groups and the countries of origin. People went out for walks while others played cards together.

Within a day the local telecommunications providers had set up some temporary phones in the entrance hall at the church. It gave us unlimited access to the outside world.

We were encouraged to call home, which most of us did. Our phone calls may have been brief, but they were reassuring. I know that many passengers offered to pay for their phone calls, but Mother Theresa reassured us that they were going to bless us. I felt sure that this was going to be a huge cost to the church.

Even from the first full day that we were at the church, both Capt. Mike and Natasha from United came to give us a daily briefing. This created a reason for us to refocus.

They kept us updated, "but not to the point of scaring anyone".

I think that this is an especially important leadership lesson that we learned. When you experience a trauma, what are you doing to help your team, your organisation or your country to refocus? Leading from the stop means that you have to reassure everyone and stop the panic from setting in.

With our recent challenges due to the onset of Covid-19 transmissions within the community, we have witnessed scenes of mass panic in the public. This has manifested itself in the panic buying of commodity items, such as toilet paper, that left supermarket shelves barren and caused fighting amongst shoppers.

I can safely state that never, throughout the whole "stop" experience did I feel a sense of panic. I believe that a lot of credit for this has to go to Capt. Mike and the crew of UA929.

From the get-go, we were informed that "the plane was OK" and that we had to divert because of "a significant incident in the US". Graphic details were not shared with us. There was no need to cause panic. We weren't lied to (we had heard that on another plane that was diverted, the passengers were told that they needed to make an emergency landing due to mechanical problems). We were simply fed the truth, as it became available during our daily briefings.

In one brief the crew shared that they had the responsibility to hand clean the plane and prepare it for passage onward to O'Hare. On another occasion, they updated us with the news that at the United HQ in Chicago, they had identified some security issues that warranted further investigation. Whilst information was scant, we were grateful for any that we received. Questions were asked by the passengers and honest answers were supplied by Capt. Mike and his crew when they could. If there wasn't a direct answer, there was a promise of an update at the next briefing.

There were times when we were given a glimpse of hope. We were told that we might be able to leave after two days there, but unfortunately that hope was extinguished by the next briefing, which happened later that day. However it gave us the framework that we needed to ensure that by the next time, if we got the green light to go, that we would be ready.

We had a list of the passenger manifest pinned to the noticeboard. We were encouraged to 'report in' to the manifest and log our comings and goings. As soon as we were 'off campus', we were to register when we left and where we were heading off to. This meant that at very short notice we would be in a strong position where we could account for every passenger.

That was important for us. We were told that we would not be allowed to depart without a full complement of passengers. It became critical for us that we stayed together as a unit. We looked after each other and we made sure that we let others know if and when we were heading out, where we were going and when we could be expected to return.

This was not a 'big brother' tracking our every move. It was more of a concerned parent sleeping with one eye open, listening for the faint creaking of the floorboards signalling their child's safe return home.

TIME TO REFLECT...

Recently New Zealand has been lifted up as a leading example of how to control Covid. We have been called the 'team of 5 million'.

When the world started to realise that Covid was a virus that could have deadly impact, we were encouraged to consider how we responded to the risk. Our Prime Minister, Jacinda Ardern, alongside the Director General of health Dr Ashley Bloomfield, gave us their daily update. This allowed us to get – and keep – focused on what we needed to do.

As a leader you may need to refocus your followers.

You may need to shift the energy from negativity and fear, to positivity and hope.

Remember that an open approach from you will garner more buy-in from your followers. If you don't know the answer, don't try to wing it. Tell them that you will get back to them, and make sure that once you have researched the question, you return with an answer.

REALIGN

The Funeral & The Escape Committee

What I hoped would be a short turnaround stretched into a five-day stay. Nobody had anticipated this arrangement, least of all the SA church we now called 'home'. Two days into our stay, we were made aware that there was a funeral planned to take place in it on Friday afternoon. [As I was researching the blogs and articles written on UA929.org, I noticed that some of my fellow passengers noted that the funeral was held on the Saturday. Irrespective of this discrepancy, we were obliged to do something!]

No alternative option was available, so we had to come up with a strategy to clean the church from top to bottom out of respect for the grieving family.

It wasn't hard enough that we were stranded in Gambo, amongst strangers, in unfamiliar surroundings. We now had to make sure that we vacated the premises for a funeral in a short time period.

Leadership always has a way of showing up. In our case, it came in the form of a Dutch man, called Montiano Blom (affectionately called 'Monti').

He gathered us into the room and started to share his vision for how we could allocate the tasks to get the church tidied up and made ready for the funeral. He asked for individuals to put their hands up to take ownership of certain areas of the clean-up, and soon he had about a dozen people (including myself) volunteering to get the job done. I smiled as I was reminded by Bob Smith that Monti got our attention with "his bowl and bloody big spoon"![17]

Without his leadership, I dread to think what impact we would have had on the bereaved family. It is safe to say that during the funeral, nobody would have suspected that 198 stranded plane people were lurking in the church's depths. The deceased was given a dignified send-off and the event passed without incident.

We had to make sure that the passengers who were using the sanctuary removed all evidence that they were squatting there. Their luggage, blankets, clothes that created the boundary of their 'space' all needed to be removed.

Floors would have to be vacuumed, cleaned and swept. Toilets needed to be sanitised. Trestle tables and chairs had to be put away or rearranged. It was a full-on military process that we had in front of us.

It was a natural thing for me to put up my hand to help. Over the previous couple of days, we made sure that we contributed as much as we could to our situation. While the Newfies prepared, cooked and served us our meals, we took up the slack by preparing the room and washing up the dishes.

It created a sense of community within the passengers. We were able to connect, strong bonds and relationships were formed.

I remember helping as we cleaned the dishes. It was my duty to dry the dishes after they were washed. There is even a picture entitled "Kitchen Krew"[8] that shows me working alongside Les and Helen. To be honest, my memory has faded about who Les and Helen were, as has my hairline!

In this situation, it didn't matter what your rank, position or title was, you just had to roll up your sleeves and dig in!

When you lead from the stop, I would encourage you to realign your team. Look for the volunteers who are willing to step up and leverage their enthusiasm. It doesn't matter what they have done before. Sometimes it's their enthusiasm that will help to pull you through.

Was drying the dishes glamorous? No.

Was cleaning the toilets alluring? Not at all! But it had to be done.

By creating order within the chaos, we managed to gain the buy-in of a lot of the passengers. It was a leader's responsibility to lead the team. We needed to get buy-in from a group of strangers to accomplish this task.

It helped that we had developed some relationships amongst ourselves.

TIME TO REFLECT...

Whatever the job is, breaking it down into smaller, manageable tasks can help!

That was what we ended up doing when we had to clean the church. For one person, the job would have been overwhelming. But by splitting it up and sharing it with a larger group, we were able to get through to completion in what seemed a blink of an eye.

But the first aspect of getting us to jump in and volunteer was the vision casting that Monti did.

As a leader, you need to be a good communicator and an excellent vision caster.

If not you, then who...?

RELAX

The Messages (From) Home

My journey to Chicago was supposed to end at a conference, where I was due to deliver a Keynote address. Despite our first 24 hours on the tarmac at YQZ, I believed that we would be back in the air and that I would still get to my destination in time to attend and contribute at that conference.

I was still in denial, as I mentioned earlier, when I entered the church in Gambo, blissfully unaware that I was going to be stuck here for a further 4 days. It took me at least 4 or 5 hours whilst at the SA before I came to the realisation that I wasn't going anywhere in a hurry.

And that, as I mentioned before, was when I decided to take my tie off... I had to resign myself to the acceptance that I was here to stay. I had no idea for how long, just that it wasn't going to be a quick turnaround.

It is easy for us (well, at least for me) to continue living as an assumed character in a play. In my case, it was the business class passenger onboard UA929. There were rules and regulations. You had to dress a certain way. The way that you acted had to be in collusion.

I realise that this will sound strange if you are reading this in 2021, or even later in time. When I started my journey in London, I was wearing my business suit, with a crisply ironed white shirt and a brand-new tie from the Tie Rack. Who can remember the last time that they travelled internationally and wore a suit and tie?

As I look back over the last decade of business travel, I would wear a tee-shirt and jeans. Maybe I would have my Red Sox jacket, or a leather jacket with me. Occasionally, I would have a less formal jacket (or blazer) with me. I would carry a pullover and, depending on the time of year that I was travelling, I might even have a thermal packed into my carry-on. The rules for travel have been rewritten.

Rules started to change from the time that Capt. Mike made the first announcement to us.

We could not leave any of our carry-on luggage on the plane.

We were not allowed to collect our stowed luggage.

We had to move on.

I spent the first day (and all night) at the SA thinking about my report. I needed to find the time to write and complete it. I needed to find the space to allow myself to pour the words out of my mind and onto my laptop screen. It became an obsessive thought.

My tie might have been removed from around my neck, but it was merely placed in the inside pocket of my suit jacket. I was still in 'character'. The first deviation from the script happened as I was waiting for that lovely grandmother to stop doting about her grandchildren.

I'm not sure what was said, or when it was said, but at some point I made a mental switch. I closed my laptop and I thought, "Elias, life is too short to worry about work."

There is a 'Far Side' cartoon, drawn by the artist Gary Larson. It is entitled "Cow Philosophy". It shows an enlightened cow, sitting cross-legged on the top of a mound of earth, wearing a red robe, draping over its left shoulder. Sitting below the mound is another, cross-legged, cow, eagerly listening in to the wisdom of its compatriot (guru). The bubble of wisdom that emanates from the red-robed cow simply states: "And, as you travel life's highway, don't forget to stop and eat the roses."

I guess that it was time for me to reset my expectations and to 'eat the roses'. I don't remember going out and enjoying long nature walks whilst in Gambo. I do, however, remember doing the dishes, cleaning up the church in preparation for the funeral, and being invited to someone's home to have a shower. We had established communication with the outside world. The phones were working and we had internet access. Life was pretty good. Bob Smith told me that he had a role in this.

I was made telephone monitor. You have no idea how guilty I felt when I had to tell folk, parents talking to kids, kids talking to parents, siblings, Grandparents etc. Your three minutes are up, please put the phone down and let the next person use it.[7]

We would make, and occasionally, receive calls. Most of the time, there was the happy chatter of loved ones reconnecting with their family. If, in the slim chance that you weren't there when an inbound call came for you, one of the team would take a message. One such message was left cellotaped to the door of the sanctuary. It was handwritten in block capitals and read:

"MESSAGE
FOR
STEPHEN MORTLAKE
FROM YOUR WIFE:
YOUR CONFERENCE CANCELLED
COME HOME"

It was such a good message that I had to take a photo to immortalise it!

By this stage I had resigned myself to the understanding that I wasn't going to be able to attend my conference. I suspected that, like Stephen, a lot of people all over the USA would be losing out on their ability to attend their conference.

The gravity of our situation didn't hit us or sink in until after we returned home. The impact of the terrorist acts on that fateful day in 2001 would send ripples across the world.

The airline industry ground to an immediate halt. Reviews on security were undertaken at breakneck speeds. TSA was redefined in the aftermath of the twin towers toppling. According to Wikipedia:

The 9/11 attacks compounded financial troubles that the airline industry already was experiencing before the attacks. Share prices of airlines and airplane manufacturers plummeted after the attacks.

Midway Airlines, already on the brink of bankruptcy, shut down operations almost immediately afterwards. Swissair, unable to make payments to creditors on its large debt was grounded on 2 October 2001 and later liquidated. Other airlines were threatened with bankruptcy, and tens of thousands of layoffs were announced in the week following the attacks. To help the industry, the federal government provided an aid package to the industry, including $10 billion in loan guarantees, along with $5 billion for short-term assistance.

The reduction on air travel demand caused by the attack is also seen as a contributory reason to the retirement of the only supersonic aircraft in service at the time, Concorde.[9]

Aviation was hit hard. US Airways entered bankruptcy on Aug 11, 2002. United followed suit on Dec 9, 2002. Even Air Canada on April 1, 2003. All a direct knock-on effect of 9/11. Tourism was also impacted. The same article (above) referenced that hotel occupancy dropped by 40%, with 3,000 employees being laid off in New York City alone.

Covid-19 has heralded a similar wave of fear and doubt. Scaremongering, fuelled by negative media reports, and supported by government intervention, has had a devastating impact on aviation and tourism. Closing of international borders, coupled with compulsory managed isolation and quarantine had an immediate impact on our national carrier, Air New Zealand. Our carrier saw flight demand shrink by 95%, wiping over NZ$5B off their forecast.

As an organisation, they projected revenues to plummet to a mere $500M per annum. Given that they had a monthly wage bill of $110M, Air NZ were looking at a 30% reduction in workforce. Their CEO went on to say that since Air NZ will be looking at releasing people, if we knew people who were recruiting, that Air NZ would be very happy to recommend them to other organisations. The reason, he justified, was that Air NZ started off by recruiting people with a 'can-do attitude'!

In 2001 despite the economic downturn, aviation and tourism rebounded. Adjustments were made as a result of 9/11. Jobs were reinstated, and life, eventually, returned to normal.

RELAX

Even with Covid-19, we are seeing the green shoots of economic recovery sprouting around us.

Maybe it is time to relax and reset...

TIME TO REFLECT...

As you travel life's highway, don't forget to stop and eat the roses!

It is time to slow down and relax. Maybe we have started to become a society that was working at breakneck speeds, unnecessary risks were being taken that could end up having devastating consequences.

With a proliferation of fake news, fear mongering was on the increase. Artificial intelligence (AI) algorithms have driven content on social media and it seems as if it is polarising us.

When 9/11 happened, the media was telling us that there was an imminent depression heading our way. Maybe even bigger than the Great Depression. They predicted it, but it never arrived.

When the Global Financial Crisis (GFC) happened in 2008, the media was telling us that there was an imminent depression heading our way. Maybe even bigger than the Great Depression. They predicted it, but it never arrived. When Covid happened, the media was telling us that there was an imminent depression heading our way. Maybe even bigger than the Great Depression. They predicted it, but it never arrived.

Maybe we should be telling ourselves that it's time to relax.

RELAX

REDEFINE

The Roles of the Locals

There were a number of local key players that were part of our story. They include:

- Claude Elliot – Mayor of Gander
- Oz Fudge – Gander RMCP (Royal Canadian Mounted Police) Officer
- Brian Mosher – CBC Reporter
- Janice Goudie – Local Reporter
- Pat Woodford – Air Traffic Controller
- Diane Davis – Local School Teacher
- Theresa Antonietti (her maiden name was Burry) – Secretary Salvation Army (SA)

I want to acknowledge what they did and how they became an integral part of making our stay in Newfoundland a positive experience. Whilst their stories have been widely shared, some of it comes through interviews that they gave to the media, and some via interviews to Zizka as part of her Masters Thesis.

The Mayor of Gander at the time, Claude Elliot, recalled his experience learning about the crisis when someone entered his office to tell him about one plane hitting the first tower and 20 minutes later, the second plane. These are Claude's words:

> *When you saw it, it's hard to believe that it was real and that it was live. It was about 11:30 in the morning, and I got a call from the town*

manager saying, you better come into the office because it looks like there's been a terrorist attack on the United States and they're going to be shutting down their airspace, and planes have been told to land at the nearest airport. Canada has agreed to take all the planes. We knew with our location and leaving Europe in the morning, once you get halfway across or over, the closet [sic] airport is Gander.[1]

Oz Fudge, a Gander RCMP officer, recollected the moment the news reached him.

I heard someone calling my name. When I looked to my right, there was Bonnie Harris. She was saying 'Oz! Oz! Turn on your radio!' I'm looking at her and I'm thinking, 'now why is she telling me to turn on my radio?' And she pulled in alongside of me and she said, 'Turn. On. Your. Radio.' I'm looking down at my police radio and she said, 'No, you fool, turn on your radio.' I go to CBC, our national radio station, and that's when I heard about the planes going into the tower. I'm thinking, 'Nah. Nah, this can't be happening. This is a joke.' I was thinking it was Orson Wells' [sic] War of the Worlds.[1]

The world was watching in horror. Everything was playing out in real-time on TV. For many watching, they believed that they were viewing a Hollywood blockbuster. With the horror unfolding in the United States, planes began to land at Gander airport (fondly referred to by its airport code 'YQX').

The locals (Newfies), like the rest of the world, expressed denial, sure that this diversion would be very temporary. Even Brian Mosher, CBC reporter, said all these planes will "be gone tomorrow morning because that was fully expected."[1]

However, as the hours wore on and the American airspace remained closed, everyone became increasingly aware that we 'plane people' would be staying much longer. Pat Woodford, an air traffic controller at YQX, remembers managing the logistics at the airport. They "didn't know how long this event was going to take before the airspace opened and everybody wanted to leave."[1] The trouble was that nobody knew exactly what the world would be like when we eventually left.

In their interviews, many described taking action to prepare the town for the coming crisis. With the state of emergency in place, Gander and the surrounding towns began to coordinate efforts to prepare their homes and spaces for an unknown number of people.

Claude designated the hockey rink as, what came to be affectionately known as, "The World's Largest Walk in Freezer." There was little time for them to pivot away from their sense of disbelief and denial, into action. Community organisations, like the Salvation Army and Red Cross were amongst the first to be called upon. Soon it became apparent that they were quickly overwhelmed. Public organisations, like the local schools needed to be engaged. Oz Fudge made the circuit around town in his patrol car.

Once the schools were onboard, they had to set up the camp beds and get everything ready for the influx of plane people. That was all done in three to four hours and was occurring at Gander Collegiate, at St. Paul's College of the North Atlantic, the churches, at the Legion, the Lion's Club, the Elks Club – all these places needed volunteers just like Gander Academy, and it got to the point where they were turning people away.

The willingness for the Newfies to help became overwhelming.

As an example, Diane Davis called six people to ask if they could come over to the school and volunteer. By the time she showed up to the school, she found 20 people there. Why so many? Because everyone was phoning someone else, telling them that they had a job for them to do. Other Newfies also described calling on all these different kinds of community organisations – private companies, service clubs, non-profits, as well as governmental and public organisations.

Without much official direction, Newfoundlanders rushed to do what they thought Newfoundlanders should – welcome strangers.

Given that some of the plane people were on their individual planes for as much as 30 hours, it dawned on the Newfies that they needed to shift their focus. As passengers deplaned, Newfies started working to alleviate passenger anxiety, confusion, and needs for information. They were no longer thinking about their own emotions and how they were coping. Their primary concern was that of the passengers'. They had experienced disbelief, and confusion after being kept on planes, some of them without information.

For many Newfies, they had to become the messenger. They regurgitated the TV footage as best they could, whilst operating in a semi-counselling capacity.

Brian Mosher remembered the disbelief of the passengers as they disembarked the planes.

> *A guy came up to me in a really expensive suit and said, what's happened? I said, what do you know? He said, barely anything, [that the world trade centre was hit]. That's true. He said, North or South tower? I said a plane hit the North and South towers, Pentagon, and Pennsylvania... He said, was there much damage? I remember his name. I said, Jim, come over by the wall and [hear] what I'm going to say. I don't know how to say it – the towers are gone.*[1]

For Newfies, they saw this moment as a turning point in how they defined their community. It was not just a place and a community in which they loved to live, but a beacon of hope and resilience. In their interviews with Zizka, they described the plane people not as strangers, or outsiders, but as members of the town, as they recollected the events. There was a phrase that kept on repeating: "We ate lunch 9,300 people. We ate supper in a town with 16,000 people."[1]

As the plane people reached their destinations, their hosts' first impressions of them was the shock, disbelief, and fear on their faces. Once they were settled in, all they wanted to do was call home.

Diane Davis outlined how they helped them armed with atlases, a globe, and a book of flags. If they did not speak the language, they would use the different mediums to determine where they were calling so that they could help the operator. This is just one example of the creative efforts community members engaged in to accommodate their guests and unforeseen barriers when structures in place would not suffice.

The phone calls only underscored the emotion of the day. Another Newfie remembers witnessing a girl having an emotional conversation with a loved one.

She was supposed to have been there on the day before and she had worked at the Twin Towers. She would have been at work that next day. Just, I think, talking to her mom or dad and getting off the phone made her just [cry].[1]

One of the local reporters, Janice Goudie, was able to listen to a passenger's recording of their pilot breaking the news to them while they were still in the air. She comments on how powerful it was to hear the gasps from other passengers in the recording of the actual words used by their pilot when they broke the news to them.

As a reporter, I'm trying not to show [a lot of emotion] in an interview but I went out to my car and I started to cry. It had gotten to a point where it was too much.[1]

Sometimes it is OK just to cry...

TIME TO REFLECT...

During times of adversity, you need to think out of the box.

This was demonstrated so powerfully when Diane Davis identifies their creative thinking to use a globe and pictures of national flags to help some plane people. These simple acts were powerful. They broke down the barriers of language and reconnected at a heart level.

At the start of the day, everybody had their 'usual' role in life. By the end of the day, these had been redefined.

Schools became hostels.

Churches fed the masses.

Stretchers, designed for military action, were redefined for alternative use by civilians in their time of need.

I am reminded of an ancient story that is documented in the old testament of the bible. It is found in the book of 2Kings, in Chapter 4, verse 2. In the story, the prophet Elisha enters the home of the widow, who is asking for his help. The prophet responds by asking two questions:

"What shall I do for you?"

"What do you have in the house?"

And the widow replies, *"Your maidservant has nothing in the house BUT A JAR OF OIL."*

Through a miracle, the prophet is able to transition that small jar of oil and fills up all the vessels that he encourages her family to borrow from the neighbours. Like the Newfies, what do you have at hand? Blankets, food, accommodation...

Stop and take stock of your surroundings and your assets and ask yourself, "How can I put these to good use?"

REDEFINE

REFRESH

Showering at Someone's Home

When you find yourself stuck in an unfamiliar place, with literally just the clothes on your back for five days, something has to give. No, I'm not talking about another wardrobe malfunction...

I was wearing my suit, with just the one pair of socks and underwear as well as the white shirt that I had on. Luckily I didn't need to wear my suit jacket, the weather, on the whole, was warm enough and, I had taken my tie off. At some point in time, I can't pinpoint when exactly, someone came in with a whole load of new underwear for the passengers to use.

Whilst I can't recall whether or not I took some for myself, I do remember that by Thursday or Friday, I was given a tee-shirt, which I gratefully swapped for my own shirt.

Throughout the area, schools were used to accommodate passengers. Attached to the gym were showering facilities. Many of the UA929 plane people were able to use those facilities. But with other plane-loads sharing that space, not everyone was able to grab a shower there. Around the same time, we had received many gracious offers from the locals to come to their homes, and use their facilities to shower, shave and generally freshen up. Once again, Steve managed to capture the essence of this hospitality for us on the UA929 website:

> *Many people were absolutely ripe until they could find a resident to offer them a shower. Several of us standing in front of the church were offered a shower at a house on day number two. It was like heaven. I found it so bizarre as I waited my turn in the kitchen of this residence. I thought*

to myself, "OK... I'm supposed to be back at work in Seattle today, yet here I am... having a conversation with some guy named Sanjay from India... in a kitchen...in Newfoundland... both of us waiting our turn for a much-needed shower". Who'dathunkit! Later on that week, a very nice lady named Rhonda did our laundry for us...and offered us bottled moose meat.[10]

We organised carloads, consisting of a Newfie as the driver and up to four plane people that we could squeeze into each car. The names of the passengers were duly noted on our lists, as was the location that they were being transported to. I remember being involved in the logistics behind this and encouraged as many passengers as possible to take up this generous offer.

The procession of cars came and left on a regular basis. I would guess that we had five or six families that opened up their homes for us. Each carload would disappear for an hour or so, taking away dirty, smelly passengers and returning with refreshed ones, renewed to continue their stay.

I waited until Friday or Saturday before I headed over in one of the convoys. It was at the insistence of others that I went. Maybe I was one of the 'absolutely ripe' people that Steve was referring to in his article! My primary focus was the wellbeing of others, so I wasn't too bothered about not going.

When we arrived at our host family's home, we were greeted with warm smiles, hot tea and a hearty hug. It felt as if we were reuniting with long lost relatives. We took our turns to jump into the shower and, whilst it was only a short shower, it was refreshing.

The biggest memory for me was not the shower, the tea, or the hospitality. It was the unnerving realisation that we had witnessed the loss of life and dignity as a result of 9/11.

I had not watched much footage of the terrorist acts on TV. Apart from seeing grainy images of the planes impacting the twin towers on TV in the sanctuary on day one at the SA, I had deliberately avoided watching anything else.

Whilst waiting my turn for a shower, I sat down with my cuppa tea and scone. Our hosts had their TV on CNN. The reporter was detailing the harrowing reports that some of the victims had called their loved ones at home and left voicemail messages. I nearly lost the plot when I started to hear the recordings. Immediately my mind raced to my wife Kay and our 5-month-old daughter Brianna. What would I have said if I had to leave a similar message? I realised that these families would never be reunited. It made me even more grateful for my situation. Until that point in time, I had bottled in my feelings and contained my emotions.

When you are leading from the stop, allow yourself the time to grieve. As a leader our primary focus is on our followers. There is nothing wrong with that. We need to look after them and to let them know that we are thinking and caring for them. John Maxwell puts it this way when he says, "People don't care how much you know, until they know how much you care!"

Make sure that you are also looking after yourself.

TIME TO REFLECT...

Who is important to you? And when is the last time that you acknowledged that to them?

I am an avid reader of books. I particularly enjoy reading self-help or autobiographical novels. One of the first books in this genre was called "The Five Love Languages". It was authored by Gary Chapman.[11]

In his book, he identifies five ways that you can show your love and affection to a spouse:
1) Through words of affirmation (telling them things like "I love you!")
2) Through acts of service (taking their clothes to the dry cleaners or making them a meal)
3) Through gifts (giving them hand-made cards or buying them a present)
4) Through quality time (putting down the newspaper and giving them your undivided attention)
5) Through physical touch (hugging someone when you meet them)

The three things that I would encourage you to reflect on, is:

1) Do you know what your love language is?
2) Do you know what your spouse's love language is?
3) Expand question two above to include your co-workers, extended family, neighbours etc...

REFRESH

RECOGNITION

Paying Attention to Individuals (The Married Couple and The Campbells)

The Gambo Salvation Army Citadel was probably the town's landmark building. It was not a grand hotel, but it can be. As a result of 9/11 it became a hostel. Theresa Burry's (that was her maiden name – she's now known as Theresa Antonietti) official title at the time was the Secretary of the Gambo Salvation Army Citadel, but during September's hospitality campaign, she unofficially became field commander. To us plane people, she was affectionately known as "Mother Theresa". As we all found out, that involved much more than the provision of food and shelter.

In a news article[12] that was aired by the CBC (Canadian Broadcasting Corporation), they captured the story about two couples who were caught in the crossfire.

Mother Theresa kicks off the story by saying, "Well Captain Reid, the Salvation Army Officer called me around six I guess on Tuesday evening, and he says, 'You need to get everything available that we have.'" She was one of the first people who greeted us plane people as we disembarked off the school buses and walked into the Salvation Army (SA) church.

We were greeted with the sight of blankets and a hall prepared for a feast for kings. Mother Theresa understood how to welcome people; it's more than food and shelter for a group. What she demonstrated was that it was about paying attention to individuals...

There were two couples in particular on our flight that she ended up noticing. The first were an Australian couple called Iain and Julia Campbell. At the time they were living in San Diego. They had their own story of September 11. The public calamity intersected with a private anxiety about their son.

By the time they arrived at the SA, they found out that their son had an abrasion on his foot and it had gotten infected. He was a professional surfer, in Indonesia at the time of this crisis. In their mind, the Campbells were considering the worst possible scenario. Their son risked losing his career with the possibility that he was going to have his leg amputated from the knee down.

Julia Campbell narrated the story during her interview for this article. "Iain and I were absolutely numb. We were walking around, totally stunned, completely helpless, you know, at some point I was beginning to feel really selfish that I had these thoughts about my own family when so many people had lost members of their family. This after all," Julia continued, "was only a limb. Theresa was absolutely marvellous. She took both Iain and I under her wing and she led us to her office. She allowed us to use her personal phone to make as many phone calls that we needed."[12]

Her husband Iain continues the story, "She also allowed us to have the privacy of the office so that we could cry when we needed to cry and, you know, felt comfortable speaking with our family."[12]

Another couple, Steve and Tara Washington, were a young couple on their way to Las Vegas to celebrate their honeymoon. Newlyweds, as newlyweds often do, got noticed.

"Steve and I found a pew to sleep on. And we realised, you know, we were going to have to face the whole night (sleeping there)," Tara explained. But it wasn't long before they were called out. A family had come to the church, having heard that there were newlyweds there. Tara went on to say that they, "basically offered up their home for us and said, you know, we will give you a bed and a shower and a bit of privacy on your honeymoon night."[12]

Local congregation members, Craig and Brenda Russell, found the stray honeymooners. Brenda picked them up at the church while Craig was out doing some rounds. When he returned home, he said that he walked into the lounge and these, "two little guys were sitting on the couch!"[12]

Tara could not speak highly enough about them. "The Russells were just fantastic. They cheered us up. They took us out, they constantly wanted to take us shopping, take us sightseeing, you know, entertain us. They brought their family to meet us. They had a barbecue for us. They wouldn't let us wallow. They just wanted us to enjoy their time, our time and Gambo."[12]

Bill Hooper, who was the Mayor of Lewisport, was also interviewed in the same article. When quizzed about what they did and what made them different, he humbly said that they just did what they thought anyone would do to make them comfortable. "We tried to be friends with all of them. I just thought everyone would do that."[12]

Newfoundlanders, Hooper went on to say, do have that reputation to try to help. When a Newfoundlander's help is needed, they generally come through when the need is there.

The reporter went on to say:

> *I can speak to this... People who drop in to Newfoundlanders are not going to go away hungry. In the four or five days of their stay in Lewisport and Gambo, the grub was ready, and often.*[12]

I can personally attest to that!

As we settled in, and the shock of events wore off, something curious occurred. We decided that we had to serenade our hosts. Another passenger on our plane, Julian Dawson, an entertainer from England, who was on his way to Nashville, Tennessee, wrote a song. He dedicated it to the people of Gambo. It was called "Waiting For A Plane"

ALL ALONG THE WATERFRONT

WAITING FOR A PLANE

A 1000 MILES AWAY FROM HOME

WE SHOULD BE PLUM INSANE

BUT OUR PLATES ARE NEVER EMPTY

LORD THEY'RE FEEDING US AGAIN

A THOUSAND MILES AWAY FROM HOME

AND WAITING FOR A PLANE

I PULLED UP TO A PICK-UP TRUCK
JUST TO MAKE A LINE OF TALK
THEY SAID NO NEED TO BE BORED MY FRIEND
WE'VE ORGANISED A WALK
WELL WE MAY BE HERE A WEEK OR TWO
BUT YOU'VE TAKEN AWAY THE PAIN
WE FEEL RIGHT AT HOME IN GAMBO
AND WE'RE WAITING FOR A PLANE

WE'RE SLEEPING IN A CHURCH HERE
LIKE WE'VE NEVER DONE BEFORE
WE'RE STRETCHED ON COTS AND BENCHES
SOME SLEEPING ON THE FLOOR
WE'RE HEADING FOR THE GUINNESS BOOK
FOR THE ALL-TIME LOUDEST SNORE
IT'S GREAT TERRAIN
WE'RE FULL AGAIN
BEEN A LITTLE RAIN
BUT WE'RE TAKING THE STRAIN
A LITTLE INSANE
BUT IN THE MAIN
WE CAN'T COMPLAIN...
WE'RE JUST WAITING FOR A PLANE

Additional verse:
NOW WE'RE BACK IN OUR OWN WORLD
WE'VE LEFT THE TREES BEHIND

OLDER AND SOMEWHAT WISER PARTS
OF THIS MESS WE CALL MANKIND
NOW EVERYTHING LOOKS DIFFERENT
IN WAYS WE CAN'T EXPLAIN
WE'VE SEEN THE BEST THAT WE CAN BE
WHILE WE WERE WAITING FOR A PLANE

Copyright © 2001 Julian Dawson

The generosity of the locals was overwhelming. They opened their homes, they emptied their pantries, fridges and freezers. They filled us with their love. They warmed us with their hot water. They enabled us to communicate with loved ones half-way across the globe.

Yet, despite our efforts to thank and repay them, we were told that was not necessary. They would not take cash so some passengers would go to the store and bought all the dry goods they could – coffee, flour, paper towels.[12]

It would be an understatement to say that we were grateful. Despite our efforts to thank our hosts, Mother Theresa sums it up best when she said, "They couldn't understand why we were so willing to open up our church, feed them, and we were doing this for nothing. We didn't want anything in return for this, and like they thought that they were in just a little village. And people could be so good so hospitable, that they were just amazed."[12]
Yes, we were amazed.

"It is what we're used to doing as Newfoundlanders," Mother Theresa went on to say. "I mean we normally are very hospitable people, so we didn't know how any other way to treat these people."[12]

TIME TO REFLECT...

Who do you need to recognise?

Is there someone in your organisation, your community or even in your family that has gone above and beyond? Are you good at spotting them? More importantly, are you good at recognising them?

They say that babies cry for it, and old men die for it. What is 'it'? Recognition!

It is a part of our humanity.

Bad leadership is the main reason that a person leaves their job (37%). 39% of employees surveyed stated that they feel underappreciated at work. A staggering 77% said that they would work harder for more recognition!

What steps are you taking as a leader to 'walk slowly through the crowd' where you work? Are you taking the time to observe others and to recognise the individuals who need to be singled out and acknowledged? Do you see those who are hurting and are you able, and willing, to do something to alleviate their pain?

We live in a world full of people who are lost, broken and in pain.

RECOGNITION

RESET

The Call To Return To The Plane

We were all anxious to leave. It seemed to be an all-consuming topic amongst the plane people.

A daily schedule of flight departures was sent to us and, pinned onto the noticeboard in the SA lobby. It was regularly scrutinised to see where UA929 was on the list. After a couple of false starts, by the fifth night, we finally got the green light that we were allowed to depart late on Saturday night.

Like a well-oiled machine, buses started to arrive. We stood alert, clipboard and pens frantically checking off individuals to make sure that none were left behind. By 2:30am, the last bus rolled out of the SA and headed back to YQZ. During a previous update, Capt. Mike had let us know that there was a security issue and as a result of the screening for the passengers in the US, we could expect that some passengers would be identified for secondary screening at YQZ. This is how Tom documented it:

> *The captain had told us that there was a security issue on our plane, which may have been the reason we were so long in departing. There were only five planes left there when we finally departed. On our flight, there were people from thirteen states and eight countries, by my count, including India and Saudi Arabia.*[6]

Imagine my concern on hearing that they wanted to pull aside a number of passengers for secondary screening. I was, after all, born in Tripoli, Libya. I spoke Arabic. Even though I was a Greek, with New Zealand citizenship, travelling on a British passport, I felt sure that I would be a 'dead-ringer' for being on THAT list.

Sure enough, we had a long wait at YQZ. After about three or four hours, they summoned us together and announced that they would be asking a selection of plane people for secondary screening. I strained to listen for the individual names. As the roll-call continued, and the names were read out, I lost count. For some reason, my name wasn't read out.

At first I thought that maybe I hadn't heard it. As the rest of the plane people scattered across the terminal, I approached the UA crew and asked if my name was on that roster. They confirmed that I wasn't. With a sense of relief and bewilderment I walked away and waited for instruction.

Bob Smith managed to give me further insight into the secondary screening. These are his words:

> *I was one of the people wanted for extra screening. I sat next to a bloke named Kifah, a Palestinian who was at the time working in Saudi, selling printer ink for HP printers, (I learned that, and some other stuff, over the five days in Gambo). On the flight before we were diverted, he had reported a hole in the fuselage next to his seat, [as] it was drafty.*
>
> *When we got back to Gander, they were worried he might have planted a gun or something in the hole. We had to wait a long time, because Canadian security in Gander didn't start work until 9AM, which is when Kifah, me and the two people in the seat in front and behind us were called in for interrogation.*
>
> *I had been in the Anti-terrorism unit of the RAF Regiment, so [I] knew the routine. When I realised what the security folk were worried about, I pointed out that if a terrorist had planted a gun in a hole in the fuselage, he was very unlikely to then report the hole. At that point they let us all board. But even so, Kifah and I got moved up to first class to keep us, (probably mainly Kifah) away from the hole.*
>
> *Steve was posted on the cockpit door with a fork or something in case Kifah should charge the cockpit. OK, now I look back and laugh at this over-reaction. But at the time of course, everyone was on edge. There was a very real fear that there could be a second wave of suicide prats on the international flights. And as we were the last flight out, maybe it was us.*[6]

It took us close to 6 hours from arriving at YQZ before we were told that boarding would be starting. We had one more task in hand. As we approached the plane, we would see our luggage on the tarmac. We were asked to locate and identify our luggage and transport them to the baggage handlers to stow into the hold.

Task completed, we were individually allowed to board and take our seats. Thereafter started yet another waiting game. Over the next hour, we saw the 'secondary screening' plane people trickle back onto the plane.

One of them happened to be a passenger who had sat across the aisle from me in business class. He was of Turkish Cypriot origin. In his late 20's/early 30's, travelling with his new bride. As he settled into his seat, I leaned over to him and asked what had transpired. He said that the first question they asked him was what he knew about floorboards. "Floorboards?" he questioned them back. "As in what we stand on?" They confirmed that was what they were asking about, to which he replied that he knew nothing.

It turns out that during the routine cleaning of the plane, the crew had identified a breach of the fuselage close to his seat and wanted to know more. There was a theory that a passenger might have deliberately attempted to interfere with the plane to hide a weapon there. Thankfully, they were able to eliminate this passenger from their enquiries. But it was what he said next that struck me the most.

"They called me by a nickname that I had at university," he told me. "That was nearly 12 years ago that I graduated." It was 2001. And the government security agencies, even back then, had a wealth of information at their fingertips. Fellow plane person, Steve, helped to confirm elements of this story when he observed:

> *After seven hours in the Gander airport terminal and a very long security check, we walked up the stairs to our huge 777 aircraft and met with the flight crew. There they were, back at attention in their uniforms once again. Captain Ballard remembered me from our conversations at the church and I had given him my business card. Unbeknownst to me, he had United Airlines headquarters verify my employment with Bellevue*

PD several days earlier.

Mike pulled me aside and asked if I could assist with a small security plan for the plane. He said that although the Canadian authorities had checked out every passenger on our flight, there was one problem. One of his crewmembers found that someone had removed a vent panel along the inside of the fuselage near a seat. They were afraid someone had dropped a weapon there before they got off upon arrival on the 11th, even though they could not see anything down inside because it went down so far. They blocked access to that row and a flight attendant sat there the entire trip. The flight attendants were visibly worried. That concerned me a bit but we were up next on the tarmac and we were ready to get out of there.[4]

TIME TO REFLECT...

Before Covid entered our lives and interrupted my routine, I was a professional speaker. One of the topics that I spoke about was "Disarming Corporate Terrorists".

Who are these Corporate Terrorists? They are your employees who are disengaged, becoming saboteurs within the organisation. They undermine the leader, working in opposition to the task ahead. If you were in a boat, the disengaged people would be rowing in the opposite direction to the way you wanted to go. Those who were actively disengaged would be drilling holes in the hull — trying to sink the boat!

Take time to reset expectations within your organisation. Saboteurs start off as engaged employees, but through a combination of 'radicalisation' by other disengaged team mates, they get frustrated and 'turn'.

Get in amongst them and help to reset their thinking about the organisation. Remind them of the vision and how they can contribute to that.

If, after your best efforts, there appears to be no change, then allow them to move on.

LEADING FROM THE STOP

RELIEF

The Emotion of Chicago

With the passengers accounted for and all onboard, we were serenaded one last time by Julian with our unproclaimed anthem, "Waiting For a Plane." It provided us with a fitting tribute that bookended our stay with the Newfies.

As we lifted off from Gander, Capt. Mike piped in the Canadian air traffic controller to one of our entertainment channels. We were able to hear them tell Capt. Mike, "Nice havin' ya here... C'mon back and see us sometime, right?"

I was exhausted and grateful for the fact that we were back in the air. It was a three-and-a-half hour flight from YQZ to O'Hare ('ORD'). It was eventful and from memory I probably slept most of the way there.

The United crew had rerouted us on to our final destinations. For some of us, it would mean flying them back to the UK where our journey had started six days earlier. For me, it meant that I would be flying to Los Angeles International airport ('LAX'), where I would connect to my Auckland-bound flight.

We were given further instructions on what would happen upon arrival at ORD. Some of us were offered access to a hotel room, where we could freshen up, have a shower or catch up on some sleep. Others were directed straight to departure gates, where they were ushered on to their connecting flights. The remainder had reached their destination and were greeted by family and friends as they arrived home.

What I hadn't anticipated was the incredibly emotional greeting that we received after we landed and taxied to our gate. As it happened, we were the last United flight to be repatriated to US soil. The ground crew were waiting for us. As I looked out of the window, I could see the firetrucks parked on the tarmac, parallel to each other. With their cannons shooting water towards the other side, they created a guard of honour for us.

I'm not an American, yet I was moved to tears by this spectacle. I wasn't the only one:

> *Our flight crew was especially affected, as I suspected they knew some of the employees on the two United flights that had crashed just days before. That greeting was a very powerful scene and the crew hugged each of the 200 passengers as they left the plane. Not your average airplane ride to say the least. Captain Ballard then called every one of the crew into the first class section for a private meeting. This was their moment and I figured it was time for me to leave. I was the last passenger off the plane.*[4]

I shared my hotel room with another passenger, who was able to shower first before they went to catch their onward flight. After I got showered and changed, I went back to the terminal and awaited the boarding call for my LAX leg.

United were gracious enough to upgrade me to first class for the remaining two legs. During the first leg, I sat alongside a portly gentleman, who worked for the Catholic Church. We had a robust conversation about God, at the time I was what I would call a 'wayward Christian'. I spoke about the other side of humanity that we witnessed through Mother Theresa and the rest of the SA congregants who had lavished us with unconditional love.

Our conversation was deep and spiritual and he convinced me to rediscover and keep my faith.

By the time we touched down at LAX, he handed me a business card and encouraged me to stay in touch. Coincidentally, I did try to email him a few days after I arrived in Auckland, but it just bounced back. To this day I could swear that he was an angel sent from heaven to look after me.

I had a few hours to kill at LAX before they gave us a boarding call for my final leg. When I entered the plane, I was asked to turn left, instead of my customary turn to the right. The seats were plush, and the meals were exquisite. But this experience was tarnished by one, small, but important feature. The crew insisted on calling me "Mr. Kanaris". It felt too formal and uncomfortable.

At one point, I got up to stretch my legs. The first-class cabin crew were by my side instantaneously, seeking to provide me with anything that I needed. "What can I get you, Mr. Kanaris?" he said.

My answer was, "Is it OK for you to call me Elias? And can you please tell me what your first name is?"

I felt that we had passed on from the formal stage and we now needed to be on a first-name, friendly basis. For me, the world had changed, and it was never going to revert back to the way that it was.

TIME TO REFLECT...

9/11 changed us forever. It is approaching 20 years since the day it happened. My son wasn't even born when it happened and my daughter was a baby, barely 5 months old. They are now young adults, navigating their own adversity in the form of Covid.

Whatever adversity you are going through, personal or professional, I pray that this book gives you a pathway to learn some of those leadership lessons from the people of Newfoundland, Canada.

We thought that many industries would close as a result of 9/11. Yet, 20 years on, they are thriving (well, at least surviving!). The airline industry has started to recover, and national travel is returning to normal. Tourism is building and with travel bubbles opening between New Zealand and Australia, we are being bombarded with increasingly familiar tourism messages from across the ditch.

Whilst life did eventually return to normal for me, it took me time to readjust and rediscover my feet. We may have to create a new 'true north', but there will be relief when it all comes together.

I'd like to leave you with one question, "What do you have to let go of, as you transition past this adversity that you are facing?"

RELIEF

REDRESS

Correcting the Wardrobe Malfunction

This story would not be finished without completing the loop...

The final hours at the SA were filled with anticipation. The atmosphere was electric.

Plane people were packing up their limited belongings, making sure that they didn't leave anything behind. Last minute sweeps were made in the sanctuary. Blankets were folded and piled up in anticipation of the Red Cross collecting and storing them for the next crisis that hit that region.

Stretchers were collapsed and stood to attention in rows, as if in formation, awaiting to pass inspection from a fictitious drill sergeant, prior to collection by the Canadian army.

The trickle of Newfies gathered pace as news filtered that we were cleared to leave. Soon they were flooding in to give us hugs and prayers for our onbound journey. Tears were shed, not because of sorrow, but genuine happiness. Mother Theresa stood tall and proud. Like a mother goose fussing for her brood, keeping them safe as they lined up behind her to cross the highway.

The buses started to fill up, and, once each reached capacity, it was dispatched.

I finally understood that I was about to be released from this phase of the story of my life. The opening verse from Bruce Springsteen's song "Backstreets" was playing in my mind:

Hey Eddie, can you lend me a few bucks
Tonight can you get us a ride

Gotta make it through the tunnel
Got a meeting with a man on the other side
Backstreeets lyrics © O/B/O Apra Amcos

I was waiting to 'make it through the tunnel & meeting with a man on the other side'.

As a member of the infamous 'escape committee', I stood beside Monti, waiting our turn before we mounted the bus for one last time. The crowd thinned in front of our eyes. By 4:00 am, the last group of plane people were instructed to board the bus.

I climbed up the steps, walked along the aisle and took a seat by the window. Next to me was my original business business class passenger. He looked at me and quietly said, "So, where is your lucky tie??!"

This adventure started on an ordinary Tuesday, except for that wardrobe malfunction. Yet it finished on an extraordinary Sunday, filled with gratefulness and indebtedness for the SA and the Newfies who had held our fragile hearts in their hands.

REDRESS

RECOLLECTIONS

In Their Own Words

As part of the research into this book, I had the privilege to speak privately to two people, who were gracious enough to take time to write down some of their thoughts.

I would like to honour them by including what they wrote here:

When I first received the call from Captain Reid, who was the office in charge of the Salvation Army in Gambo, that I was to start to plan to have 198 passengers stay at our church, my very first thought was "they are going to be hungry, what are we going to feed them". I started with phoning the leader of our women's ministries group and asked her to call the ladies from the church and start preparing soup, sandwiches and something that people can have with a cup of tea or coffee. She got to work on the phone chain and getting food prepared, I then went to the local grocery stores and picked up all the toothbrushes, toothpaste, soap and deodorant that I could find as I was told, the passengers are only coming with their carry-on luggage. We then waited for what seemed like an eternity to greet these strangers to our church. Someone one asked me, weren't you afraid that one of these passengers could do something to hurt all of you? I can honestly say, that thought never, ever entered my mind.

One of the very rememberable moments for me during the stay of our now "new friends" was when I received a phone call from our head office telling me that Walmart had graciously donated a skid full of men's and ladies' underwear. However, I had to try the best I could to get specific sizes, so I thought the only way for me to do that was to get the names and sizes of underwear. So off I went out in the corridor with my pen and clipboard where the passengers lined up to tell me as privately as they could what size underwear they would need. I remember very specifically, as a well-known Christian author, Jill Briscoe coming very quietly "I will need size medium britches, please."

Just 10 months prior to this horrific tragedy, I became a widow and now lived alone. So who better could offer their house for a shower house. The passengers use to take my car and go to my house to shower all day long. I remember receiving a phone call at the church from my own house, with one of the ladies asking me if it was ok to put the towels in the washer for the next group of people who were to arrive.

My life was changed from this event. I had the opportunity the next January to go down to NYC to volunteer at ground zero and that was the beginning of my work with The Salvation Army Emergency Disaster services, which my husband and I are quite involved in to this day.[13]

Theresa Antonietti (nee Burry) Former Secretary, Salvation Army, Gambo

It's really strange to think how events in our world, no matter how far away, can have a deep lasting effect on us as people. Sometimes things that seemed to be so far away can have a lasting effect on us, almost as if they happened in your own back yard.

On September 11, 2001 my day began like any other day. The world around me was settling into a fall routine as summer began to come to a close. Like most days I headed to the local coffee shop to see my regular group of friends and to chat about the happenings of the day. By mid-morning I would hear about the tragic events in the United States and before we would reach lunch time, I would come to realize that this was no ordinary day, especially when you're the mayor of Gander and Gander Airport was about to get extremely busy.

The events in the wake of September 11, 2001, that would occupy Gander and the towns that surrounded it were enormous. Gander, with a population of 9,300 at the time would welcome almost 7,000 guests with

no notice or preparation time. Yet, in the events that could have been perceived as impossible, we rose to the occasion and provided the stranded passengers with memories and hospitality that would place us on the world stage as an example to others. Through our giving Newfoundland heritage, we would care for our guests in a spirit of loving and caring that the world would come to know as amazing.

The scripture tells us that "we should always do onto others as you would have them do onto you". It also reminds us that "if you do good deeds to others, it would come back to you, tenfold". I truly believe this to be true.

In a time of need there is no better feeling than to know that someone, even a person you had never met before, truly cares about you. This was basically the approach of the citizens of Gander and the surrounding towns for the days that followed September 11, 2001. The needs, worries and care of others became ours. Through it all strangers became friends and then became family to us.

I've spoken to groups on this subject countless times. Through the amazement and captive eyes of any of the audiences, I always remind them that "human kindness will always overpower hatred and on the day when the world was shown the worst of humanity, we somehow were able to show the world the best of humanity".

Did I ever expect this to end up being told in a major Broadway musical that would be seen around the world? Not in my wildest dreams. Remember, September 11, 2001, began as just another ordinary day.[14]

Claude Elliott, Former Mayor – Town of Gander

REFLECTING

A Final Thought

Being in the middle of a crisis sometimes means that you cannot see the wood for the trees. However, this doesn't mean that you should soldier on and ignore the learning lessons.

What were the lessons that we could learn from 9/11?
Where could we apply this to Covid-19?

One of the Newfies was a lady called Diane Vey-Morawski. Her husband worked with the Canadian armed forces. When she was interviewed by Zizka, she made the following observation:

> *All peacetime military does is exercise, training, and exercise. When we do exercises, they'll come up with a scenario, and some of them are almost like a small novel and there's quite a bit of character development in a creative situation and sinister plots... We have little scenarios based on that and we respond accordingly. If someone had come up with this, we'd say come on guys get real, that's a little outlandish.*[1]

Are we producing our own playbook of scenarios for our lives or for our businesses? Do we have that mini novel that allows us to predict a 'whatif' scenario? Have we planned for a disaster occurring?

I live in Aotearoa/New Zealand. It is often referred to as "Godsown". It is such a beautiful country that I have heard people joke that when God goes on holiday, He comes to New Zealand! But New Zealand is also a land of geological diversity. We are prone to earthquakes, and have experienced volcanic eruptions.

The Civil Defence authority in New Zealand encourages us to be prepared. We are encouraged to get our homes ready, our work ready, even our schools/communities. What have you been doing differently to get yourself ready for another crisis?

There were a couple of things that became apparent for me as a result of my 9/11 experience. The first was a direct result of 9/11 being a passenger on flight UA929. On the first anniversary of the attack, I called in to our local Talkback Show on radio where the host of the show, Leighton Smith, asked me to share my experiences.

I told him how we had to (eventually) evacuate the plane and were instructed to take all of our carry-on luggage with us. Whatever we had checked in remained in the hold of the plane. As a result, we ended up wearing the same clothes that we had on at the start of our journey. In my case, the only item that I had in my carry-on luggage was my laptop and various documents that I had been compiling during my business trip. Living in the same clothes for over 5 days can soon lose its appeal!

Smith asked me whether I had made any changes to my travel habits? Indeed, I had! For a start, I made sure that I always packed a spare set of clothes, including underwear, and had space in my carry-on bag for toiletries. If possible, I would make sure that I wore comfortable shoes that could double up for exercise as well as business use. Try living off the same clothes if your luggage fails to arrive with you at your final destination.

Thankfully there has only been one instance when I had to make an emergency trip to a clothes store to buy new clothes as a result of baggage handling issues. I'm grateful that in every situation I was eventually reacquainted with my luggage!

The second thing that I became aware of is that for far too many people, we live without enough margin in our lives. When I interviewed my friend and founder of MIOMO (Making It On My Own), Yvonne Godfrey in April 2020, she offer the following viewpoint about margin:

> ***Well, I think the first thing is to do a total regroup on what assets you have. So that's financial assets (or not), and that is the sadness about all***

of this is that everyone's taking a financial hit. And on that, I would say, and I don't mean this to be in any way condemning, but I know with the families that I work with, that most people do not have enough margin in their lives. So, they don't have enough financial margin. They don't have enough time margin, but they have enough thinking margin. And what that means is the margin is the excess. That's why a book is not written to the edge of the page, because we visually need space around that to be able to take in the words.

And so when we look at where we're at right now, it's about saying, Okay, what is the margin that I have and if it's not enough, then write a huge note in your diary, tattoo it on the inside of your eyelids to say, "I must live differently in the future so that when times of famine come (and this is literally what it is) that I have something in the storehouse". And I'll guarantee you that Air New Zealand, apart from being 52% owned by the government has a lot in the storehouse to take them through this time. Big organizations generally do.

But the sole trader or the small business owner, or the employee may not have enough margin. So we can't get more margins that we don't already have right now. But we can plan differently for the future. And remember, life is all about the future. How are we going to do this differently? So that's number one.

Number two is: "What can I do? And how can I do it, maybe differently?" So, it's about assessing one's assets in terms of skills, in terms of ideas that you've had. There may be an idea that has been latent for a long time, like it was with me with the MIOMO program. I had been in the Amway business for 30 odd years, before I transitioned into doing MIOMO. And I was terrified, because that's all I had known from the age of 22. I was 54 when I started MIOMO. That's 32 years of experience. 32 years of reputation. 32 years of comfort of familiarity and 32 years of income at a very nice level. Thank you very much and the passive income.

Now the passive income that I had from Amway was what gave me the freedom to have a go at building MIOMO. And once again, there was my margin. However, I still didn't have the guts to do it until I was *pressured from without. In other words, people started to put pressure on me to do something with this. So, this is one of these occasions right now, where there is pressure from without. In other words, all around us, we're having to reinvent ourselves, we're having to rethink. So, I would encourage our listeners today to say we are all in the same boat, and those that make the most of the future will be those that have the courage to do this reassessment today. Of what is it that I have? What is this arrow in my quiver that I've not yet used?*

What can I now turn into something magical while other people are possibly in fear or sitting on their hands, or blaming or whatever they're doing? Because this is stages of grief that we're at. We are all in stages of grief right now, having lost what we thought was stable, what we thought was what we could do and having to turn it into something new.

So, assess what you have. And then if you're if you're a believer, if you're a Christian, you go right to the source and say, "Lord, how can I turn this thing you've given me. that I may not have used, this idea or this talent or the skill? How can I now turn it into something that will bring value to others and that will create an income for me?"[15]

My encouragement to you, dear reader, is to think through how you can create more margin in your life. Please take the time now to take inventory of your life and your possessions.

Do you have enough put aside for that rainy day? Or are you just living from paycheque to paycheque?

Do you have enough time put aside for you to go out there and 'smell the roses'? Or are you running from task to task, oblivious to the consequences that might have on your health?

Are you investing in your relationships? Or are you side-lining them to your work (or other gods that you are worshipping)?

We only have one life here on earth. It isn't a dress rehearsal. Use this time wisely. Another crisis will befall you. It's not a case of 'if', but 'when'. And when your world seems to come crashing down to an absolute halt, remember three things:

1) You're not in trouble
2) We believe in you
3) We're here to help

As I think back to the tragedies of September 11, 2001, I want to thank the Newfies for being there in our time of need, and supporting us. Me. You. We.

Let me leave you with two Māori words: "Kia kaha!" That means, "Stay strong!"

ABOUT THE AUTHOR

ELIAS KANARIS is an author, professional keynote speaker, executive coach, leadership trainer, and entrepreneur. He has been a regular keynote presenter and he has frequently spoken to audiences in the I.T., telecommunications, insurance, financial services, real estate, and education sectors across thirteen countries on four continents.

Born in North Africa, he had to learn to adapt when, at the age of 8, his family emigrated to establish a new life in London, England. He had to learn about a new culture, adjust to a different cuisine and integrate with others who had distinct accents. Elias left the UK to travel to the other side of the world, re-establishing himself in New Zealand in his early 30's.

Elias has been a senior consultant in the I.T. and Telecommunications sector. He was part of a team responsible for his company's top twenty-four clients, which billed $450 million per annum. Elias is also a founding partner of the John Maxwell Team (JMT) – the largest and fastest-growing leadership training organisation in the world, serving on the President's Advisory Council (PAC). Elias served as the National President for the Professional Speakers Association of New Zealand (2015-2017). He also served as President of the Global Speakers Federation (2018-2019), a US$4 Billion industry that represents Professional Speakers globally.

Elias was a passenger on flight UA929, bound to Chicago O'Hare from London Heathrow, when his plane became one of 38 that was diverted to Gander airport in Newfoundland, Canada. When his world seemed to stop in a heartbeat, Elias had to dig deep into his store of resilience to navigate through this new normal.

Elias now lives in Murrays Bay in Auckland with his family. Leading from the Stop is his third book.

WHERE TO FROM HERE

Going through a crisis can be a stressful time for anyone. Whether it is domestic abuse, loss of a loved one, loss of a job, or during times of uncertainty, remember that you don't have to journey alone.

Below are a number of resources that you can head to where you can find a community that you can belong to or access to valuable support systems that are in place.

If you want to seek some resources on counselling, please head over to https://www.lftsbook.com There you will find links and resources to help you with your journey.

We encourage you to join our FB community at https://www.facebook.com/leadingfromthestop. You can join this like-minded community where we will encourage you to share the positive changes that have happened to you as a result of reading this book.

Finally, if you would like Elias Kanaris to speak at your organisation, please feel free to reach out to him here: https://www.eliaskanaris.com/contact.

How to contact Elias Kanaris:
www.EliasKanaris.com
Elias@EliasKanaris.com
Phone: +64 (0) 9 280 4420
www.LeadingFromTheStop.com

ENDNOTES

1) You Are Here: Narrative Construction of Identity and community resilience in Newfoundland during and after 9/11 by Laine Cosette Zizka
2) Steve's story (part 1) https://ua929.org/content7fcb.html
3) Bob's story https://ua929.org/content7267.html
4) Steve's story (part 3) https://ua929.org/content1ada.html
5) Bob's story (continued) https://ua929.org/content097b.html
6) Tom's story https://ua929.org/contenta36d.html
7) Private email sent by Bob Smith to Elias Kanaris
8) The "Kitchen Krew" https://ua929.org/gallery6cfd.html
9) Economic effects of the September 11 attacks Wikipedia https://en.wikipedia.org/wiki/Economic_effects_of_the_September_11_attacks
10) Steve's story (part 2) https://ua929.org/content0233.html
11) Gary Chapman "The Five Love Languages https://www.amazon.com/Five-Love-Languages-Heartfelt-Commitment/dp/8186775099/
12) CBC Interview https://www.facebook.com/Iainsurfer/videos/10212427766801057
13) Private email sent by Theresa Antonietti to Elias Kanaris
14) Private email sent by Claude Elliott to Elias Kanaris
15) Yvonne Godfrey interview with Elias Kanaris https://vimeo.com/404153101